discovermore

Exploring Life Science

# Food Webs and Food Chains

Ernest Brazzos

Britannica Educational Publishing

IN ASSOCIATION WITH

THE ROSEN PUBLISHING GROUP

Published in 2025 by The Rosen Publishing Group, Inc.
2544 Clinton Street, Buffalo, NY 14224



Editor: Brianna Propis
Book Design: Michael Flynn

Photo Credits: Cover Annette Shaff/Shutterstock.com; (series background) Dai Yim/Shutterstock.com; p. 4 (deer, lion) SaveJungle/Shutterstock.com; p. 4 (grass) Quarta/Shutterstock.com; pp. 5, 21, 25, 27 BlueRingMedia/Shutterstock.com; p. 6 Deckar 007/Shutterstock.com; p. 7 aiyoshi597/Shutterstock.com; p. 8 Followtheflow/Shutterstock.com; p. 9 Doug McLean/Shutterstock.com; p. 10 Aitor Lamadrid Lopez/Shutterstock.com; p. 11 Piotr Zawisza/Shutterstock.com; p. 13 (top) Romas_Photo/Shutterstock.com; p. 13 (bottom) The Jungle Explorer/Shutterstock.com; p. 14 Martin Pot/Shutterstock.com; p. 15 Alexander Canas Arango/Shutterstock.com; p. 16 Kanyshev Andrey/Shutterstock.com; p. 17 Diane Isabel/Shutterstock.com; p. 18 Stephen Mcsweeny/Shutterstock.com; p. 19 (berries) KPixMining/Shutterstock.com; p. 19 (rabbit) FullframeFactory/Shutterstock.com; p. 19 (fox) Harry Collins Photography/Shutterstock.com; p. 20 Guitar photographer/Shutterstock.com; p. 22 Damsea /Shutterstock.com; p. 23 Barou abdennaser/Shutterstock.com; p. 25 (top) Michael Vi/Shutterstock.com; p. 26 karl umbriaco/Shutterstock.com; p. 28 Watchares Hansawek/Shutterstock.com; p. 29 A. Michael Brown/Shutterstock.com.

**Library of Congress Cataloging-in-Publication Data**

Names: Brazzos, Ernest, author.
Title: Food webs and food chains / Ernest Brazzos.
Description: [Buffalo] : Britannica Educational Publishing, [2025] | Series: Discover more! Exploring life science | Includes bibliographical references and index.
Identifiers: LCCN 2023051655 (print) | LCCN 2023051656 (ebook) | ISBN 9781641901598 (library binding) | ISBN 9781641901581 (paperback) | ISBN 9781641901604 (ebook)
Subjects: LCSH: Food chains (Ecology)--Juvenile literature.
Classification: LCC QH541.14 .B7334 2025 (print) | LCC QH541.14 (ebook) | DDC 577--dc23/eng/20231222
LC record available at https://lccn.loc.gov/2023051655
LC ebook record available at https://lccn.loc.gov/2023051656

Manufactured in the United States of America

Some of the images in this book illustrate individuals who are models. The depictions do not imply actual situations or events.

CPSIA Compliance Information: Batch #CSBRIT25. For further information contact Rosen Publishing at 1-800-237-9932.

# Contents


Food = Energy .......................... 4
Autotrophs .......................... 6
Herbivores .......................... 8
Carnivores .......................... 10
All-Eaters .......................... 12
Scavengers Eat What? .......................... 14
Decomposers Eat What? .......................... 16
Forest Food Chains .......................... 18
Grassland Food Chains .......................... 20
Underwater Food Chains .......................... 22
Desert Food Chains .......................... 24
An Ice-Cold Food Chain .......................... 26
A Broken Link in the Chain .......................... 28
*Glossary* .......................... 30
*For More Information* .......................... 31
*Index* .......................... 32

# Food = Energy

Food is important to the survival of living things because it gives them the energy they need to live, grow, and move. When a deer eats leaves, it gets energy from that food. When a lion eats a deer, it takes in energy stored in the deer's body. Energy flows from one living thing to another when it is eaten. This can be shown as a **food chain**.

## WORD WISE

**A FOOD CHAIN DISPLAYS A LINK OF ANIMALS THAT FEED ON LIVING AND NONLIVING THINGS, IN ORDER OF WHO EATS WHOM.**

## Consider This

Do you mostly eat vegetables or meat? Do you eat a lot of both? Where do you think you'd be on a **food web**?

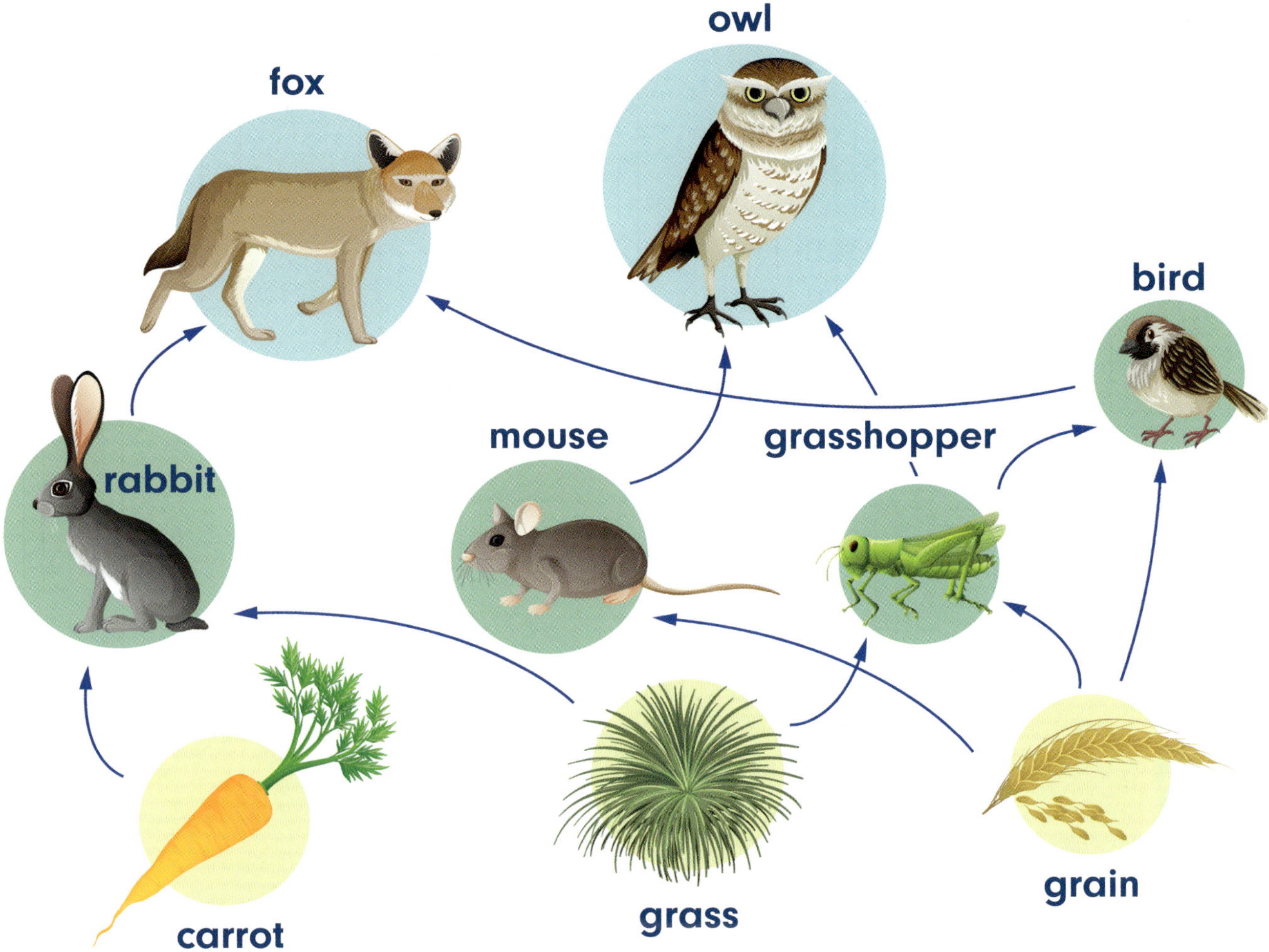


## WORD WISE

A FOOD WEB DISPLAYS NUMEROUS FOOD CHAINS, IN ORDER OF WHERE ENERGY FLOWS THROUGHOUT EACH ONE.

# Autotrophs

Some living things don't eat food for energy. Plants make, or produce, their own food. That's why they're known as autotrophs, or producers. Plants use water and a gas called carbon dioxide to make food in their leaves. This is called photosynthesis. Plants get energy for this process from sunlight. The sun is the first thing at the beginning of every food chain and food web.

A plant's leaves are like its factories for food production!

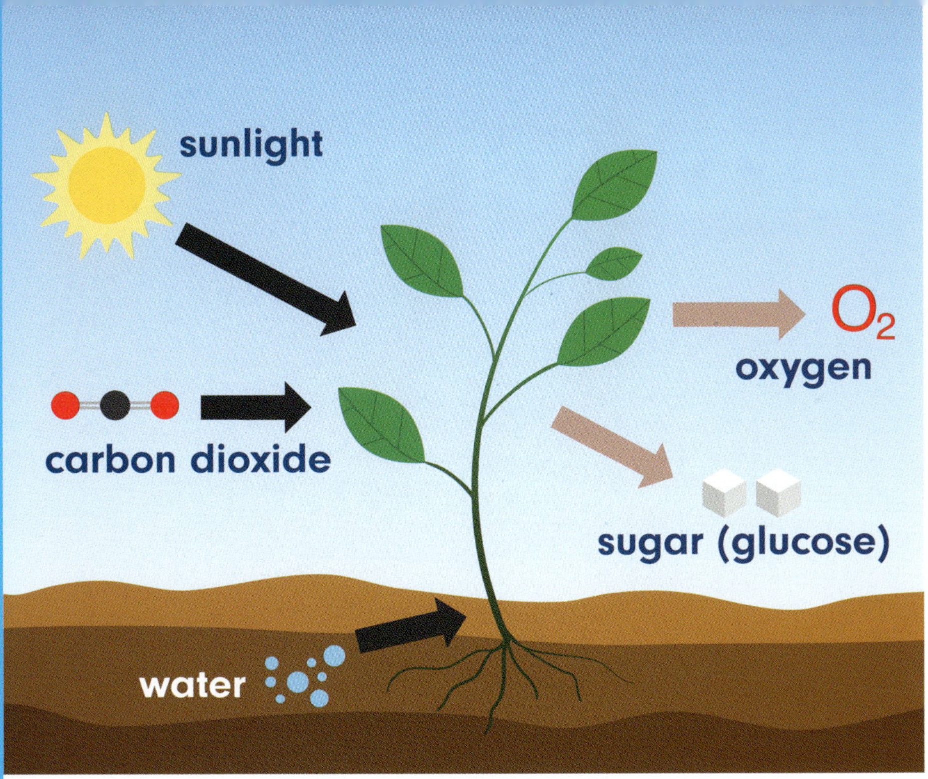


This diagram shows the process of photosynthesis.

Plants take carbon dioxide from the air and light from the sun into their leaves to create food. They take in water through their roots. Green matter in the leaves, called chlorophyll, traps energy from sunlight. The energy turns the gas and water into sugar and oxygen. Sugar, called glucose, is stored by the plant to use as food. Plants release oxygen into the air, which animals need to survive.

## Consider This

What do you think would happen to a plant that was kept in the dark with no sunlight?

# Herbivores

Everyone you know is a consumer—your family, friends, and yourself. Even your pets are consumers! Consumers are living things that consume, or eat, other living things to get energy. Animals that eat plants are called herbivores. Herbivores are the second link in a food chain or web. Photosynthesis gives them the energy they need to live and move, which is stored in plant parts.

Plants produce sugar in their leaves, and they send it to their roots, seeds, stalks, or fruits for storage.

Some herbivores, such as deer, enjoy eating fruit.

Herbivores may eat an entire plant or certain parts of a plant, such as leaves, to receive energy. Butterflies feed on the sweet nectar made in flowers. Mole rats dig underground and eat plant roots. Pandas eat bamboo stems, and chickadees eat seeds.

## Consider This

Herbivores, such as buffalo and cows, have strong and flat teeth. Their teeth are not pointy or sharp. How do flat teeth help the animals get energy from eating plants and grass?

# Carnivores

Wolves, sharks, and mountain lions are all meat-eating consumers, or carnivores. Some carnivores eat herbivores. For example, wolves eat grass-eating deer and coyotes eat rabbits. Some carnivores eat other carnivores, too. For example, sharks eat seals, which eat fish. The larger in size a carnivore is, the more options it has to eat!

Certain carnivores—such as bearded vultures—will eat the bones of their prey.

Spiderweb fibers are five times stronger than steel of the same width!

Carnivores have special body parts and functions to help them snatch prey. These include sharp teeth and good eyesight. Sea turtles have spikes in their mouth to catch slippery jellyfish. Spiders spin webs to catch flies. Owls have better eyesight than humans do and can see better than them in the dark!

## Consider This

Did you know that some plants, such as the Venus flytrap, eat meat? Although it's rare, some plants get nutrients from small animals, such as insects, frogs, and rodents. Why do you think these plants evolved to need meat to survive?

# All-Eaters

If you eat fruits, vegetables, and meat, then you are an all-eater—or an omnivore! Omnivores are consumers that eat both plants and animals. That includes not only meat but also other foods that animals produce, such as milk or eggs. Some omnivores have features for eating different foods. For example, bears have sharp front teeth for cutting and chewing meat, and flat back teeth for grinding plants and fruits.

Piranhas are fish that have very sharp teeth and are known for feeding on other animals. However, they also eat underwater plants. Many animals eat both plants and meat to survive when the place where they live changes. For example, grizzly bears survive cold winters by hibernating and eating mostly grasses and fruits to store energy when meat is scarce.

An orangutan's diet is nearly 90 percent fruit, but they still occasionally eat eggs and small vertebrates. So, they're omnivores!

## compare and contrast

A raccoon is an omnivore, and a wolf is a carnivore. Even though they both eat meat, how do you think their teeth might be different?

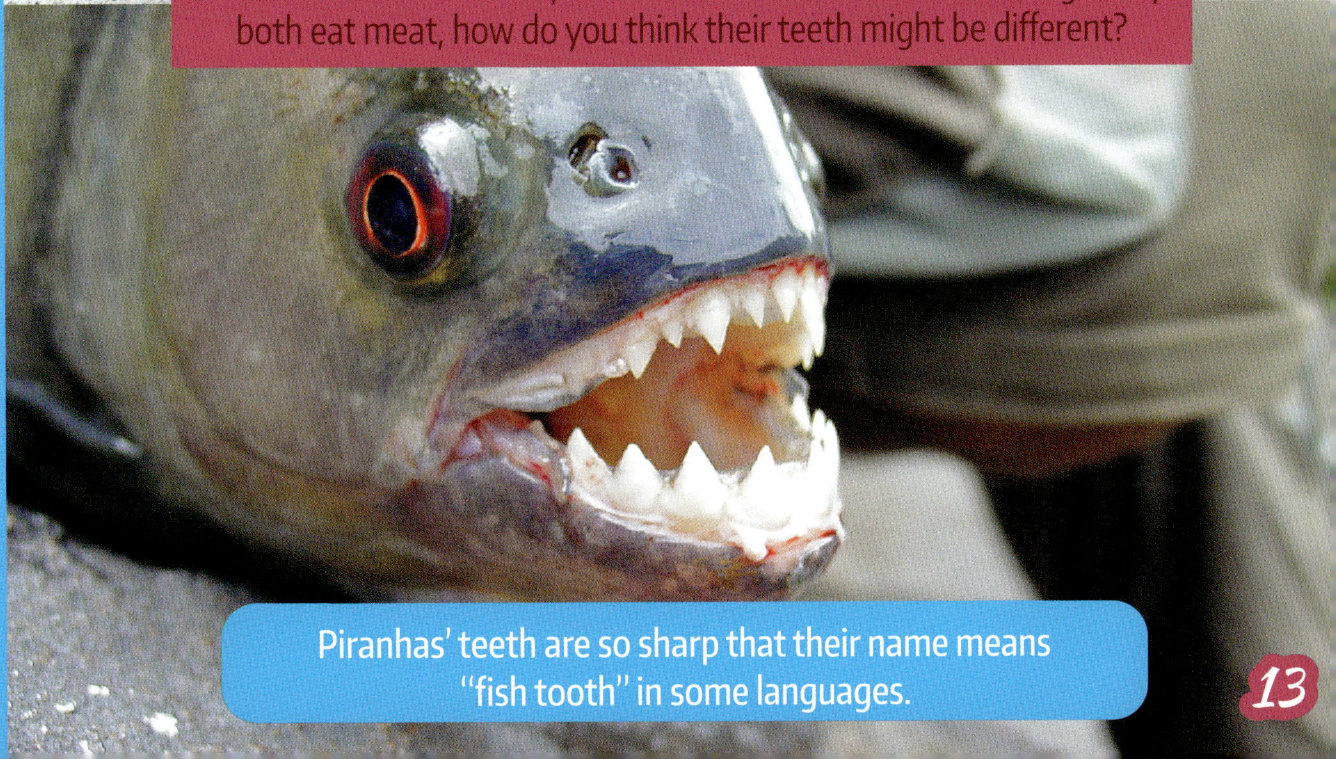

Piranhas' teeth are so sharp that their name means "fish tooth" in some languages.

# Scavengers Eat What?

Scavengers eat rotting meat and plant matter, often from dead animals and plants. Crabs, eels, vultures, and blowflies are all scavengers. Some carnivores scavenge when they can't hunt. For example, lone hyenas eat the bones of dead animals, but packs of hyenas hunt together. Scavengers often use their strong sense of smell to locate rotting flesh.

Blowflies often feed on the wounds of animals. The animals can still be alive and healthy.

Be careful if you're eating food outside near a seagull! Seagulls are known to steal food scraps because it's easier for them than hunting.

Scavengers and decomposers work together when consuming animals. Scavengers help to clear away the remains of dead animals, and decomposers take it from there.

## Consider This

It's more common today than it was in the past for seagulls to live near cities and towns. Why do you think this is?

# Decomposers Eat What?

Decomposers are the final links in food chains and food webs because they feed on the remains of living things, from dead leaves to pieces of food left over by scavengers. Examples of decomposers include fungi, such as mushrooms, and tiny living things called bacteria. When blowflies leave behind their larvae on a dead animal, the eggs hatch and maggots spread bacteria over the body as they feed on it.

Fungi release chemicals called enzymes that decompose dead plants and animals. Enzymes help break down the remains so fungi can absorb their nutrients.

Without decomposers, dead animals, insects, plants, and animal waste would pile up everywhere!

Bacteria are an example of decomposers that break down waste and animal remains for nutrients. Nutrients are substances that all living things need to live. Rain washes nutrients into the soil. The nutrients help more plants to grow. Therefore, new food chains and webs can begin as decomposers **recycle** nutrients back into an ecosystem.

## WORD WISE

**RECYCLING IS THE PROCESS OF CONVERTING WASTE INTO NEW, USEFUL MATERIALS.**

# Forest Food Chains

Food chains exist in all ecosystems, such as a forest. The main producers in forests are trees. These plants have strong, thick trunks that hold up many branches and leaves. Animals consume many parts of trees. Deer eat bark, caterpillars eat leaves, and monkeys eat fruit. Coyotes, spiders, and hawks are consumers that hunt prey in forests.

Hawks hunt by flying over fields or watching the ground from a high perch and swooping down to catch prey with their talons.

Leaves fall to the forest floor from trees when they die. Scavengers, such as woodlice and millipedes, eat this waste. Fungi decompose what is left and release nutrients when they do. This makes the surrounding soil rich and helps tree seeds grow into new trees.

Foxes living in forests get their food energy partly by eating rabbits. Rabbits eat the berries and leaves of plants, which make their own food by photosynthesis.

## compare and contrast

Many places in the northeast United States experience snowy winters and hot summers. How might a forest's food chain in this area be affected by the change in weather and temperature throughout a given year?

# Grassland Food Chains

Tough grasses are the main type of plants that grow in grasslands. Grasslands are too dry for many trees to grow there. Grassland herbivores have adapted to get energy from grasses. For example, **ruminants** such as cattle have four stomachs to digest the grasses.

Cows consume about 2 percent of their body weight, or 24 pounds (10.9 kg), in grass per day.

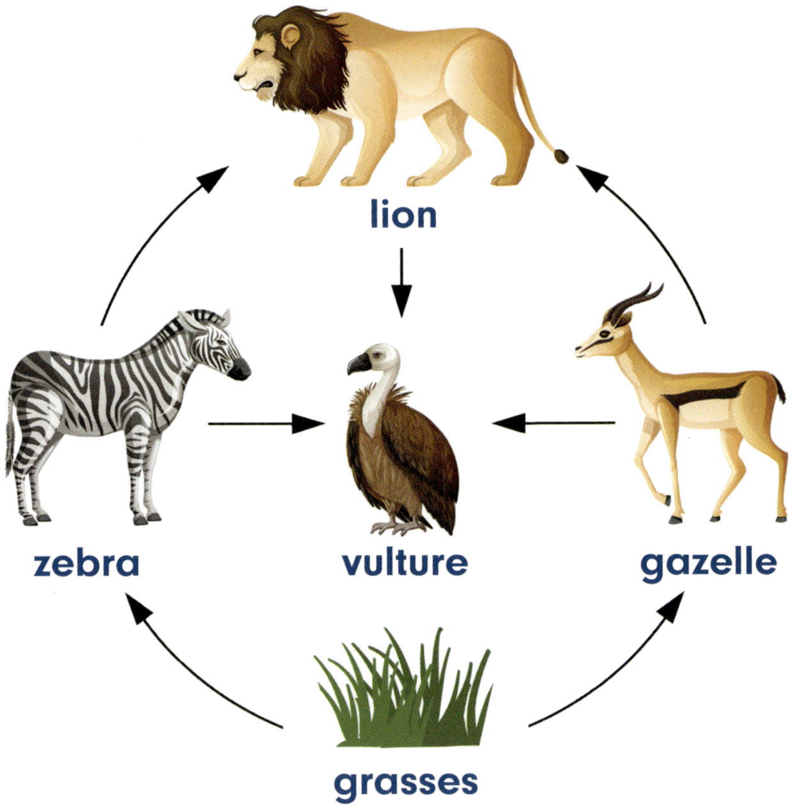


This diagram displays a typical food web in the African savanna.

Larger grassland predators, including lions, cheetahs, and hyenas, hunt grazing animals, such as zebra and antelope. Grasslands also include tiny ticks that climb from the grass onto animals to suck their blood. Scavengers that feed on animal remains and waste, such as vultures and dung beetles, are also an important part of grassland food webs.

## WORD WISE

**RUMINANTS ARE MAMMALS WHOSE STOMACHS ARE DESIGNED TO EAT AND DIGEST PLANTS AND GRASS.**

# Underwater Food Chains

Food chains also exist underwater in the ocean. Ocean food chains and webs begin with plantlike living things called algae. Like plants, algae make their food by photosynthesis. Seaweeds are algae. There are also billions of very tiny algae in the sea. Animals such as baby crabs and jellyfish eat the algae. Baby sea creatures are also eaten by a wide range of fish, such as sardines and sharks.

Photosynthesis is not as easy for plants to conduct underwater. However, algae in the ocean developed a protein that helps them to collect the light they need from the sun.

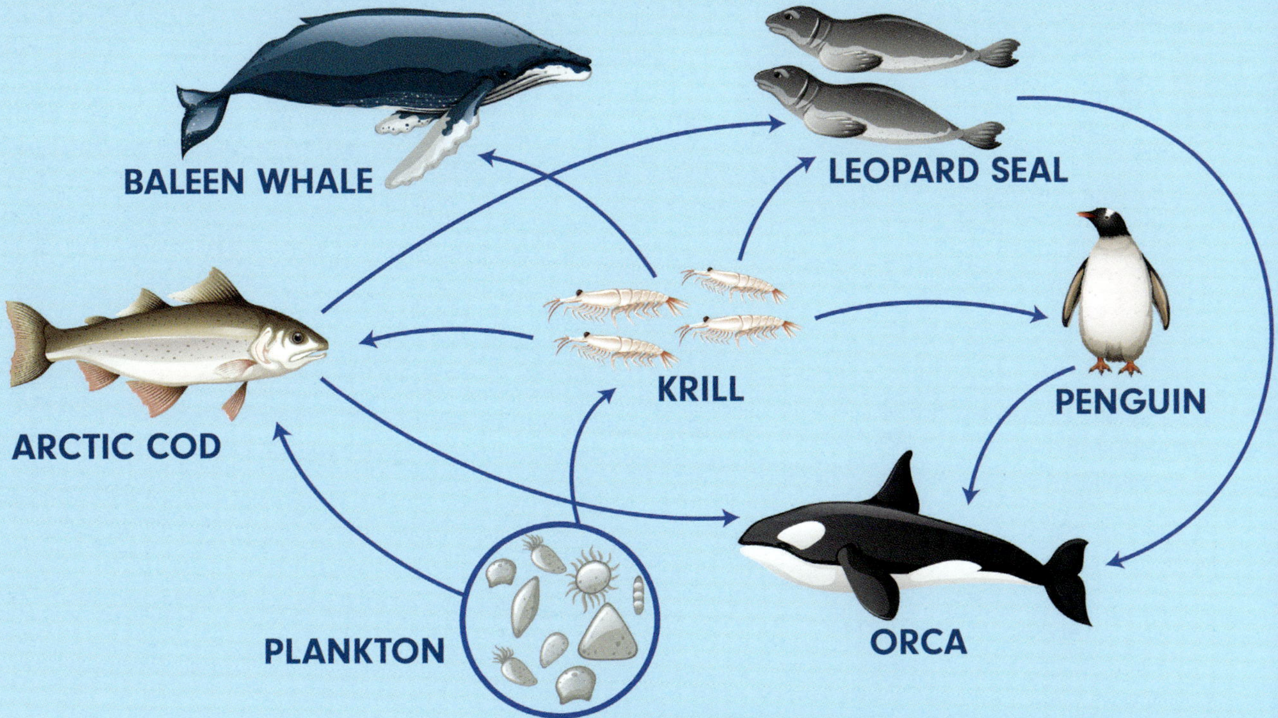


This diagram shows a typical ocean food web.

Many ocean animals, including octopuses, squid, and dolphins, feed on fish. These animals may become prey for sharks and whales. Dead ocean animals sink to the seafloor, where they are eaten by eels, spider crabs, and other scavengers.

## Consider This

Scientists classified blue whales and great white sharks as endangered and vulnerable, respectively. What would happen to the ocean food chain if these species became extinct? How might humans play a role in this?

# Desert Food Chains

A desert is a large area of land that receives little to no precipitation, or rain, throughout a given year. In a desert near the equator, it's boiling hot by day and freezing cold at night. The biggest desert plants are cacti. Whenever it rains, cacti swell up to store water inside their tough stems. Their leaves are tough spikes, which prevents many animals from eating them. Herbivores—such as antelope, ground squirrels, pack rats, gerbils, and camels—eat desert plant parts, such as cactus flowers and grass seeds.

Many desert animals are nocturnal, or most active at night, because the temperature is cooler. Carnivores have different ways of finding prey in the dark. Rattlesnakes can sense the heat that prey such as mice make. Barn owls have exceptional hearing and can find prey by sound alone.

The white-tailed antelope squirrel is a desert omnivore. It feeds on seeds, insects, and mice.

## compare and contrast

Desert animals have adapted to the strong heat and lack of water in the desert. Some do this by storing fat—which raises their body temperatures—in their tails or humps rather than in their entire bodies. What are some other ways desert animals have adapted to the heat that animals in other areas, such as the ocean, wouldn't have to?

This illustration shows a typical food chain in the desert.

# An Ice-Cold Food Chain

The Arctic is an ocean surrounded by land around the North Pole. The temperatures there are freezing cold for much of the year. Algae grow under ice that floats in the Arctic Ocean. Small ocean animals, such as shrimp, eat these algae. Fish, such as Arctic cod, then eat the shrimp. Seals, seabirds, and whales eat fish and other animals, including crabs. When seals come to the surface to breathe through holes in the floating ice, polar bears kill and eat them.

Lichens, mosses, and small shrubs are the only producers that can survive on Arctic land. Caribou and enormous, shaggy musk oxen are the largest animals that eat these plants. Packs of Arctic wolves hunt those herbivores for food.

Arctic wolves hunt in packs. They often seek out prey that is old, sick, or weak.

This is an Arctic food web on land and in the ocean.

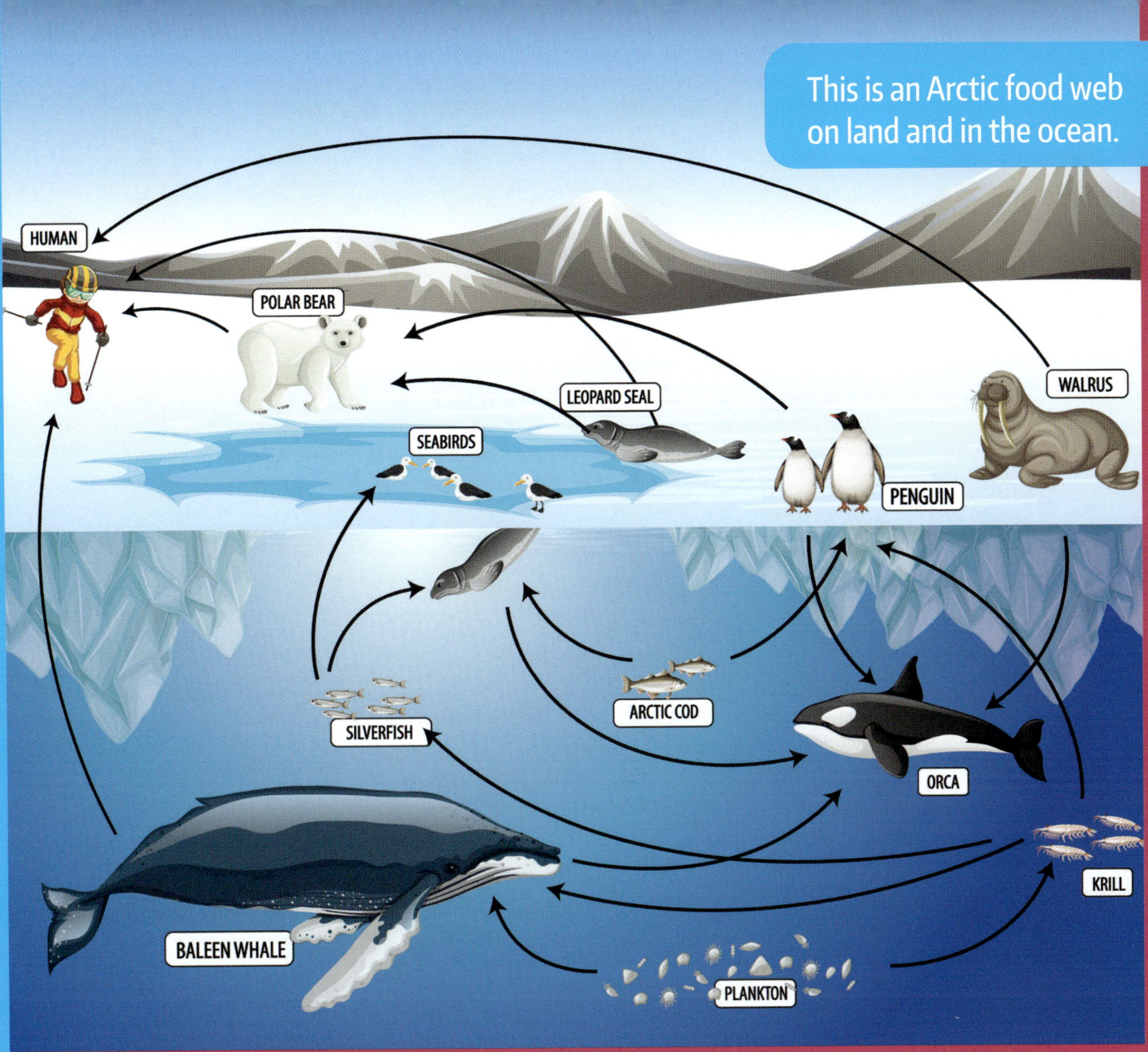


## Consider This

The Arctic is warming three times faster than the global average. How does this affect the animals that live there? In what ways will the food web be harmed?

# A Broken Link in the Chain

Each part of a food web and chain impacts the other parts, even if they're not directly connected. When one type of animal is killed, it affects other links in the food chain or food web. People cause changes when they hunt animals, turn forests into farmland, or bring new animals to a place. For example, farmers brought cane toads to Australia to kill beetles that ate their crops. But the toads killed other animals that ate them because they have poisonous skin. This has harmed the food chain.

When people catch too many fish or hunt too many deer, they change the balance in food chains and webs.

Wildlife preserves are natural areas of land or water created for the protection and study of certain animals and plants. Hunting is banned from these areas.

We can help food chains and webs by protecting the places where plants and animals live, being aware of the resources we use, and educating ourselves on wildlife needs. We can protect living things by making it against the law to hunt or harm them. What can you do to protect natural food chains and webs?

## Consider This

If an animal becomes endangered in the wild and members of its species are placed in a wildlife preserve, how could this protect the animal from becoming extinct?

# Glossary

**carbon dioxide** A colorless, odorless gas found in the air.
**digest** A body process that breaks down food.
**ecosystem** A group of living things that exist with each other in an environment.
**endangered** Any type of animal or plant that is in danger of becoming extinct.
**evolved** How a species changes over time.
**extinct** The dying out of a species from Earth.
**grassland** An area of land covered mainly in grasses.
**hibernating** When an animal conserves energy by slowing its heart rate and eating very little. They do this to survive cold winter months.
**lichen** A small plant made up of an alga and a fungus living together.
**maggot** A wormlike baby fly that feeds on rotting animals, plants, and waste.
**protein** A molecule that helps the body do important functions.
**resource** A material that humans need, such as land, air, and water.
**species** A group of similar living things that can reproduce together.
**vertebrate** An animal with a backbone.
**vulnerable** A species that is likely to become endangered.

# For More Information

## Books

Eason, Katherine. *Big Cats: And Their Food Chains.* Shrewsbury, Shropshire, UK: Cheriton Children's Books, 2023.

Hansen, Grace. *Food Chains.* Minneapolis, MN: Abdo Kids, 2020.

Hansen, Grace. *Food Webs.* Minneapolis, MN: Abdo Kids, 2020.

## Websites

**Khan Academy Food Chains & Food Webs**

*www.khanacademy.org/science/ap-biology/ecology-ap/energy-flow-through-ecosystems/a/food-chains-food-webs*

Learn about how food chains and food webs represent the flow of energy and matter.

**National Geographic Food Chain**

*education.nationalgeographic.org/resource/food-chain/*

Learn about a variety of different animals and their feeding habits through informative articles and intriguing videos about food chains.

**National Geographic Food Web**

*education.nationalgeographic.org/resource/food-web/*

Learn about a variety of different animals and their feeding habits through informative articles and intriguing videos about food webs.

Publisher's note to educators and parents: Our editors have carefully reviewed these websites to ensure that they are suitable for students. Many websites change frequently, however, and we cannot guarantee that a site's future contents will continue to meet our high standards of quality and educational value. Be advised that students should be closely supervised whenever they access the internet.

# Index


## A
Arctic, 26, 27

## B
bacteria, 16

## C
carbon dioxide, 6, 7
carnivore, 10, 11, 14, 24, 26
chlorophyll, 7

## D
decomposer, 15, 16, 17
desert, 24, 25

## E
ecosystem, 17, 18
enzyme, 16
extinction, 23, 29

## F
forest, 18, 19, 28
fungus, 16, 19

## G
grassland, 20, 21

## H
herbivore, 8, 9, 10, 24, 26

## M
marine life, 22, 23
meat, 5, 10, 11, 12, 13, 14

## O
omnivore, 12, 13, 25
oxygen, 7

## P
photosynthesis, 6, 7, 8, 19, 22
protein, 22

## S
scavenger, 14, 15, 16, 19, 21, 23
sugar/glucose, 7, 8
sun, 6, 7

## T
teeth, 9, 11, 12, 13

## W
water, 7
weather, 19, 24, 25, 26